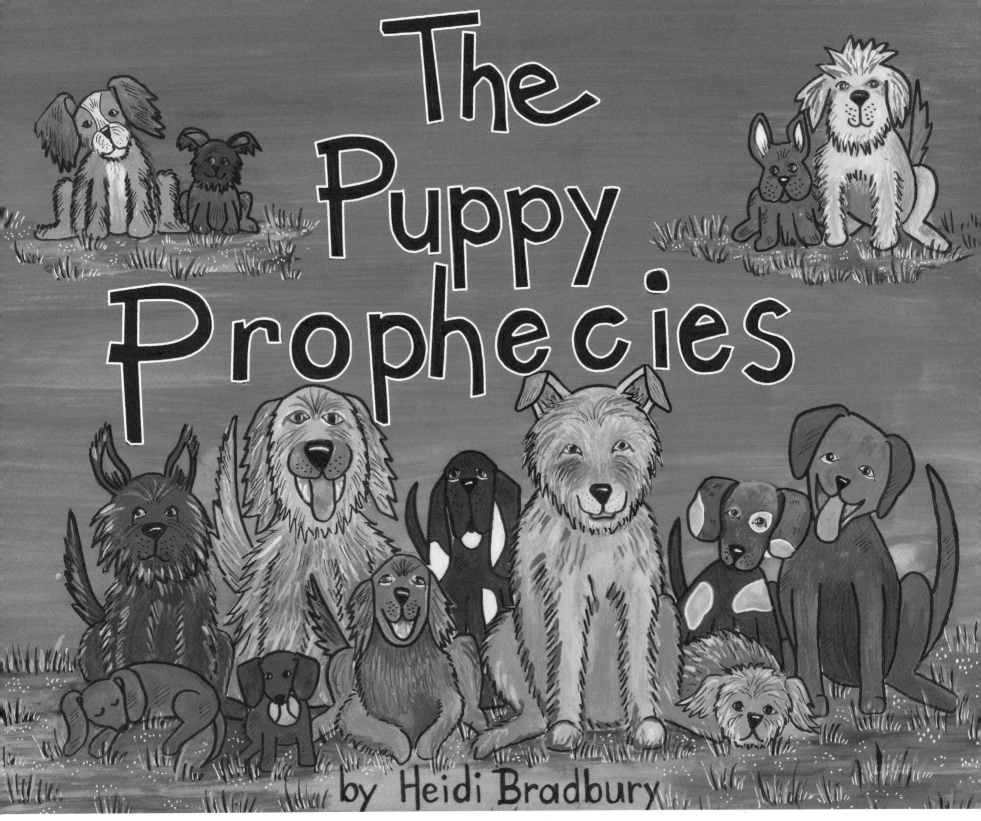

The Puppy Prophecies

by Heidi Bradbury

ISBN

Print: 978-0-692-19591-8

Published in the United States

Ojai, California 93023

heidibradburyfineart.com

Book design by Ojai Digital

Written and Illustrated by Heidi Bradbury

Best Wishes
Heidi Bradbury

The oldest and clearest records of the man and dog relationship appear in paintings and inscriptions carved in stone in ancient Egypt five to six thousand years ago. In **The Puppy Prophecies** we flash forward several centuries to learn of the mischief our wonderful companions are up to today.

All dog lovers have endless stories and incredible images in their head of the special things their companions do daily to make them smile, laugh and love them more. Hopefully these pages will bring back special memories and bring you closer to your beloved canine friends.

"It is amazing how much love and laughter they bring into our lives
and even how much closer we become with each other because of them."

– John Grogan

"If you don't own a dog, at least one,
there is not necessarily anything wrong with you,
but there may be something wrong with your life."

– Roger A. Caras

I can explain everything.

I chewed up all your sneakers.
Now you never have to leave home again.

"When was the last time someone was so overjoyed to see you,
so brimming with love and affection that they literally ran to greet you?
A dog will do that for you - ten, twenty, thirty times a day."

– Lionel Fisher

"I have found that when you are deeply troubled,
there are things you get from the silent devoted companionship of a dog
that you can get from no other source."

– Doris Day

Nothing in the world is friendlier than a wet dog.

"You can usually tell that a man is good if he has a dog who loves him."

W. Bruce Cameron

"I've always had this feeling that all dogs are therapy dogs."

Meg Donahue

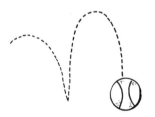

"No matter how little money and how few possessions you own, having a dog makes you rich."

– Louis Sabin

It's hard
to make ends meet

"A dog is the only thing on earth that loves you more than he loves himself."

– Josh Billings

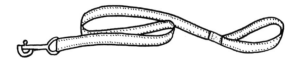

First we steal your heart.
Then we steal your bed.

"The better I get to know men, the more I find myself loving dogs."

– Charles de Gaulle

"Number one way life would be different if dogs ruled the world: all motorists must drive with head out window."

– David Letterman

"The best therapists have fur and four legs."

– Unknown

"Dogs are loyal friends, and if they could talk, your secrets would still be safe."

– Richelle E. Goodric

"Everyone says they have the best dog, and none of them are wrong."

– W. R. Purche

"The journey of life is sweeter when traveled with a dog."

– Unknown

Bone Appétit

"Happiness is:
listening to your dog snoring."

– Unknown

"All his life he tried to be a good person. Many times, however, he failed. For after all, he was only human. He wasn't a dog."

– Charles M Schulz

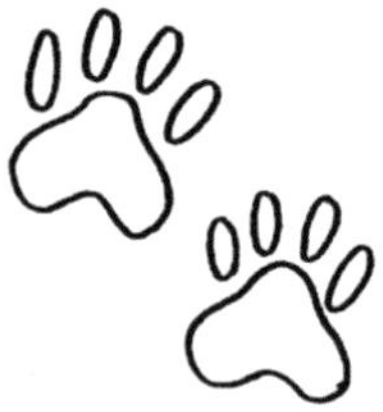

About the Author

Heidi Bradbury is an artist, teacher, and a children's book author and illustrator.
She lives in Ojai, California with her husband, Mike and their children, Michael, Sean, and Heather.

Heidi can be contacted at heidi@heidibradburyfineart.com.

CPSIA information can be obtained at www.ICGtesting.com
Printed in the USA
BVIW12n1756251018
530514BV00006B/11

* 9 7 8 0 6 9 2 1 9 5 9 1 8 *